My Father's Barn

Bernadette McCarrick

Introduction

The barn stands a few yards from the dwelling-house in its red roof and door, its whitewashed walls and gable. In my father's time, which spanned almost a century, the barn was his domain: a roomy, neatly-kept storehouse for the countless resources useful to farming life long before the age of mechanization.

The double door was wide enough to take a cart. On wet days my father worked there sawing sticks for firewood, mending the teeth of broken rakes, or oiling his beloved bike. You could always step into the barn out of a heavy shower, or keep watch for the bread-van on a cold evening through its one small window. Decades ago, on summer nights, the neighbours borrowed the safe-keeping of our barn for the kettles and pots they used for cooking their dinner on the nearby bog.

This book of poetry is a barnful of memories: a simple storehouse for the experiences of farm and family life during my childhood in the fifties and sixties. It focuses on my father, Harry who died on Saint Stephen's Day 2008, a few weeks after his 97th birthday.

About the Author

Bernadette McCarrick has published in Ireland and the USA. She has won several awards for individual poems in the last twelve years. She was poetry editor for the *Cistercian Studies Quarterly*, and was short-listed for the Hennessy Literary Award for emerging poets, 2007. This book is her first collection. Originally from South Sligo, she now lives in Balbriggan with her husband Kevin.

Contact Author: myfathersbarn@gmail.com

Acknowledgements

I need to say a word about a literary resource which I have used as a format for many of the poems in this book, namely the **Haiku**. Haiku has a long history, but very simply, it is a Japanese form. Its gift is brevity. It consists of three lines of 5 syllables, 7 syllables and 5 syllables respectively. In Japanese a poet can say a lot more in those 17 syllables than can a poet working in English. A haiku has a specific purpose: to capture a moment in the world of nature. In my usage of haiku in this book, however, I have taken liberties with that purpose. I have asked haiku to tell short stories, take snapshots, record sounds and celebrate vignettes from the milieu of nature and human nature alike which surrounded me in my native place and particularly in the person of my father. I enjoy the discipline of the limits of haiku, and marvel at the distilled drop of life that it yields.

Secondly, I need to acknowledge the resources of memory, and of family members as the wellsprings of My Father's Barn. The faculty of memory itself is a miracle, but it is never perfect or whole. David Ebershoff in his novel The Nineteenth Wife, says *I feel I must say a few words about memory. It is full of holes. If you were to lay it out upon a table, it would resemble a scrap of lace.* I realize that my mother, brothers and sisters each have their own 'scrap of lace' to lay out upon their own table of memory. I am very grateful to them for encouraging and respecting mine.

Special thanks is due to my mother Brigid and to my father Harry who gave us all a great store of words and expressions, and shared with us the many poems they knew by heart from their schooldays.

I thank my brother Frank for proofreading and his help with the text, and my brother Pat for his sound advice, and his work on the book cover.

Contents

In memory of my father
Harry McCarrick, 1911-2008

Farming

'And as I was green and carefree, famous among the barns
About the happy yard and singing as the farm was home'.

Dylan Thomas

Signal

In the beginning
A white sheet spread
On a hedge at the house
Beckoned him home
From tillage-field
Meadow or bog.

Until

There was a child
Old enough
To bring him a note
Instead
Which said:

Harry, come to your dinner.

Harry, come to your tea.

B.

Sabbath

After the milking
He hefted
Ten and twelve-gallon
Creamery-cans

On to the turf-barrow,
Wheeled them
In the bog-road
To the summer stream

And lowered them
One at a time
Into the cooling
Waters of Sunday,

Until Monday morning
When Paddy Coleman's
Creamery cart
Came round again.

After Cutting Turf

On the evening
Of the second day
He would complain
Of *tálach*.

My mother took
A strip of flourbag
And bound together
The two middle fingers

Of his right hand
To ease the pain
As she did each year
After the turf was cut.

Tálach: A gaelic word which means cramping and swelling of
the wrist

Horsetracks

On the beach where the sand is
Soft on Sunday morning
I walk in the wake of cantering horses.

Their shod hooves have left tracks
At intervals and depths as perfect
As the cupped hollows

My father made with the loy
On the brown tillage-field
At home.

Here in the presence of horsetracks
I step into the moment
When I follow him up the ridge

Placing the split seed-potatoes
Into the dark pockets
He has made, and again

When he overtakes me
On his way down
Smothering them happily

With the back of his coin- bright spade.

I am From

I am from bare cement floors
And open hearth fires in the beginning.

I am from latches on doors
And pounds of butter wrapped and left
To keep cool on the parlour floor.

I am from dressers loaded with delf
And buckets of fresh spring water
Carried from the well.

I am from home-baked bread
And bacon and cabbage for dinner
And cally and rice-pudding on Fridays.

I am from wellies
And knee-socks with patterned tops
That folded down over
Home-made elastic garters.
I am from pinafores and hand-knit jumpers
And sturdy brown shoes
You polished on Saturdays.

I am from bicycles for every journey.

I am from small fertile fields
Bordered by briars and hawthorn hedges.
I am from wild strawberries
And blackberries picked
From ditches of moss.

I am from bog and heather and turf
And back-breaking saving of turf
And turf fires in the range.

I am from meadow
And the tall grasses of summer
And blistering saving of hay.
I am from pitchforks and rakes and ropes.

I am rhubarb tarts at meadow time.

I am from rosaries at night in the kitchen
And musical nights with the gramophone
And all the old seventy-eights.

I am from falling asleep
To the voices of visiting neighbours
Downstairs,
And the sound of Delia Murphy
Singing *What will you do love*
When I am going......

How to Lap Hay

First,
Bend and gather
The full of your two arms
Of damp hay
In a clean sweep.

Next,
Shake it airily
To the ground again
In small amounts
To make an orderly pile,
Making sure to place
The wettest wad on top.

Bend again.

Now,
Lift the entire armful
Folding it loosely
Into a round bundle.

Finally,
Set it on the stubble
With exquisite lightness
And pray for a fresh breeze
To dry it
To sweet perfection.

Saved Without Rain

Mow it.
Let the sun
Shine on it.

Shake it.
Let a breeze
Blow through it.

Rake it.
Let the fine night
Season it.

Gather it
Into windrows.
Let it sweeten

To a crisp
And fragrant hay
For winter fodder.

Cartrope

The coiled cartrope
Long and heavy
Was kept under the stairs.

Used for tying
Loads of hay and oats
To the cart

For the bringing in,
Come October we tied it
To the beech tree

And made a swing.

Fair Day

Brown-paper parcels
Swing-dangle from
Handlebars and carrier.
Daddy is home
From the fair!

Four o'clock finds him
Soaking his tired feet
In a basin of salted water
By the range

Recounting cattle
And every bargain
Of the last twelve hours
He has made or overheard:

The dealer who walked away,
Only to return
To settle price or luckpenny
And swore, *Not a penny more!*
And spat on his palm at that.

Oh yes. And all the swindlers
He had met, the swiggers
Of porter. The scoundrels
Squandering their good money
In public houses on drink

When by right
They should have been
At home by now
Carefully taking the string
Off their brown-paper parcels

And sharing out the spoils.

Scarecrow

'But on well-run farms pests have to be kept down'.
Seamus Heaney

To frighten the pestering crows
Away from his new-sown oats

My father made an example
Of one unfortunate crow

He shot with the double-barrel gun
And hung

Out on a stick
At the top of the oatsfield,

Her upside-down wingspan
Flapping in the breeze,

And scaring to death
More than just her fellow crows,

But setting his mind at ease.

All in a Day's Work

Rise in the early morning,
Breakfast and say a prayer.

Plough a field with two horses,
Mow a meadow by scythe.

Shear the sheep of their fleeces,
Deliver a cow of her calf.

Follow a fox and shoot it –
The one that had taken the lamb.

Plant a field of potatoes,
Harvest a crop of oats.

Cut back a hedge with a slash-hook,
Hang a gate at a gap.

Mend all the broken fences,
Gather up all the tools,

And when it comes to evening,
Sing while milking the cows.

Your Stack of Oats

You did your farming all day on your feet.
You saved the turf, and then the hay by hand.
The neighbour said your stack of oats was sweet.

You mowed the meadow, kept the headlands neat.
You fenced your fields, and fertilized the land.
You did your farming all day on your feet.

Year on year, the seasons would repeat.
The weather would be *terrible* or *grand;*
No matter what, your stack of oats was sweet.

You gave your children an occasional treat:
For summer play, a cart of river sand,
And you did your farming all day on your feet.

Now bring them calves a load of hay to eat,
And count them cattle in the field beyond –
It was for them your stack of oats was sweet.

Now you can rest. Your tasks are all complete.
How many decades did you work the land?
You did your farming all day on your feet.
The whole world knows your stack of oats was sweet.

My Father's Barn

You open the door.

You get used to the dark.

You see:

A selection of buckets, two rakes and a spade,
Three pitchforks, the hedge-knife, the scythe,

That ladder he made, the turf-spade, the loy,
The shovels all propped in their place,

The twister he fashioned for the making of ropes
From a spooled bucket-handle he bent,

The clippers, the hatchet, the hammer, the shears,
The crosscut, the scythe-stone, the oil,

The folded manure-bags, the file and the blades,
The saw and the binder-twine rolls.

You smell the potatoes, the bog and mown grass,
Old coats on the back of the door.

You step out.

The home-made bolt is difficult.

You get used to the light.

All creatures Wild and Tame

The Cows

In nineteen fifty-five
Mick Kivlehan our neighbour
Helped my father build
A cowhouse for twelve cows.

Each had her own name
And due-date for calving
Written in a small notebook
Kept in the cabinet drawer.

Tagged and vetted
He walked them to river and field
Where they grazed and lazed
Until evening

When they browsed their way
Homeward, heavy with aftergrass,
And milk. Each cow
Went to her accustomed stall

An arm going round her neck
To tie her chain
While she flicked at clags
And midges with her tail.

Calving Time

'It seems she has swallowed a barrel'.
Seamus Heaney

On a raw evening in Spring
Just at the growing of the light

My father would say, *That cow*
Will calve before morning.

Her bones are down. He'd set
The clock for three, and like

A man getting up to a child
He'd sleepily check on the cow

Spreading out fresh straw,
Leaving ready a knotted rope

For the calf's front feet.
Sometimes the calf arrived

Unaided, behind his back.
Sometimes it was a long haul

Of ropes and broken nights.
One year there were twelve bull calves.

Beastings

After the cow calved
She had the privilege
Of warm mashed feeds

Hand-mixed in a bucket
For three days in a row.
Did that make up

For removing her calf
Unseen, to a small
House bedded with clean straw?

Did it make up
To the mother cow
For dipping your fingers

Into the first milking
Of her beastings, and
Offering them

To her bewildered newborn
Who lunged at you hungrily
Until it tasted her, and then

Couldn't get enough?

Haiku

A mink in the henhouse
Terrorizes the pullets
Bloodsucks every one.

*

After the fox
Breast-feathers float in the sky
Four fine hens dead.

*

A plump cock-pheasant
In his fabulous plumage
Dead by the roadside.

That songthrush we watched
Smashed the snail-shell open
On a big flat stone.

*

Warm summer evening
Eleven freshly-shorn sheep
Rest under their tree.

*

Lambs bleat for three days
Confused by their strange mothers
After the shearing.

October evening:
Twin brown-and-white calves
Graze the half-acre.

*

Weanlings all sold
Their hooftracks still sheltering
In the lee of the hedge.

*

Stopping at the gate
Six cows lift their heads mid-munch
To stare at us.

Strangely, at three
The cows bellow to come home.
By four, a sudden storm.

*

Cattle wintering out
Their countless watery hooftracks
Full of moonlight.

*

Among the tall weeds
In a discarded kettle
We found a wren's nest.

Bernadette McCarrick

Craftsman

Bernadette McCarrick

Grandmother-of-Pearl

His grandmother's gift
When he was eight years of age:
Her mother-of-pearl
Rosary beads.

Over the decades
He restrung them twice
With the finest copper wire.
He hung them

On a cup-hook in the kitchen
And took them down
Morning and night
For prayers.

Buttonholed

The girl who sat beside him
In Carrowmore school said,

I'll do the sums for you
If you do the buttonhole for me.

'Right so', said he.
'Give me the needle and thread'

Haiku

Good with the needle
He patched his knee-worn trousers
Darned his heel-worn socks.

*

With hammer and brads,
Sharp knife, leather, last and awl,
He resoled our shoes.

*

For the bar of his bike
He made a small padded seat
To carry a child.

The Ballad of Father Christmas

Santa got tools and timber.
Santa went to the loft
And in his spare time he fashioned
A wooden wheelbarrow apiece
For two small boys.

Santa got colours and brushes.
Santa painted the lot,
And on a dark evening he finished
A sturdy wheelbarrow apiece
For two small boys.

Santa crossed to the barn door.
Santa undid the bolt,
And in the horse-trap he secluded
A coloured wheelbarrow apiece
For two small boys.

Santa waited 'til Christmas.
Santa crept into the house,
And placed in the waiting kitchen
A ribboned wheelbarrow apiece
For two small boys.

Santa was having his supper.
Santa was saying, *Whist?*
I think I hear Santa Claus moving.
I wonder what did he bring
For you small boys?

Santa said, *Open the door!*
Santa watched his two boys
And waited until they discovered
A magic wheelbarrow apiece:
Santa's first Christmas toys.

Baskets

For basketwork
He cut red rods
From the roadside
At Templehouse.

In the tank
By the hayshed
Home-grown sallies
Were long steeping

Becoming more supple
By the day, while
On the dresser
Copper-fastened hoops

Shaped to perfection
Waited for ribs
And woven rods.
On basket-making days

We walked through
Curled rod-parings
In the winter-dark
Kitchen where he worked

So that by mid December
The porch was full
Of varnished willow-baskets
With elegant handles

And dogwood stripes
The colour of ripe plums
(Courtesy of Templehouse).
Each basket rocked

Delicately to the touch
Like little cradles
Made ready for the holding
Of Christmas,

And before we knew it
The house was Bethlehem-full
Of the gift
That was our father.

Glimpses

Bernadette McCarrick

Haiku

For doing the jobs
He tied his old coat round him
With blue binder-twine.

*

He taught us balance
Going with him up the bog
In the horse-drawn cart.

*

On winter evenings
While he was feeding the calves,
He rubbed their backs.

I have jobs to do
He'd say, when he got tired
Of the visitors.

*

Those glasses he wore
Bought at the fair for ten bob
Were once his father's.

*

On a child's birthday
He'd fish a warm half-crown
Out of his waistcoat.

Hung on a nail
Above the back kitchen door
His bicycle clips.

*

All Ireland Sunday
He cycled to the boarding-school
To pay our fees.

*

River-flooded road
The bike ferryman brought us
Across for school.

At night, the stories
Of characters he had met
During the day.

*

After Sunday Mass
Sixpenny ice cream for him
Tuppenny for you.

*

Tea on the bog
Old coat spread on the heather
For comfort.

Music on a childhood
Summer evening: my father
Sharpening the scythe.

*

Backload of hay
Awkwardly crossing the fence
To five hungry calves.

*

On the upright
At the bottom of the stairs
His old woollen cap.

Sunhat-happy
In his July-warm garden
Picking blackcurrants.

Five Decades
27 June, 1995

They have five gold coins between them now.
The first is the morning sun
Rising over Knocknashee,

Circling the Moy at noon
And setting over the Ox's rim
At evening milking-time.

The second is the harvest moon
Hung above sheaf and stook
And hardwon turf and hay in sheds.

The third is a golden crown
For seven little heads of curls:
Four boys, three girls.

The fourth is a round brown
Cake, baked and buttered
And shared at their kitchen table.

The fifth is a story written down,
A song, a poem, a tune
The fiddle plays on winter nights.

Five gold coins they have:
One for every decade, grown
From the half-sovereign
That he gave her on a day in June.

Bernadette McCarrick

Neighbours

Bernadette McCarrick

Two Sonnets for Kate Gilmartin

(1)

All the handiwork began with Kate.
She taught my father all she knew of rods
When he was a boy of seven or eight -
A time when people carried home their spuds

And turf by basket, or a pair of creels.
Kate was the one who passed him on the art:
How to grow the rods, and all the skills
Of bending seasoned willows, and the part

Where you shaped the hoop and ribs, and tied
Them fast, then filled the frame with weave.
The talent of the artist never died.
She gave my father all she had to give.

The craft was shared before it was too late.
All the handiwork began with Kate.

(11)

When Kate Gilmartin got a fleece of wool,
She finger-teased it out 'til it was fine
Enough to spin. After the spinning wheel
She carded it, and rolled it up like twine.

While working on a fleece, her hands were full
Of industry, and oily thread. Her time
Went into knitting, and she turned the heel
On many a sock – socks that were the kind

You'd wear in winter when your feet were cold.
They bore the colours of an onion skin,
And softer hues of sphagnum moss, I'm told
With which she dyed the wool, and in the end

When Kate Gilmartin died, her house was full
Of unworn socks that felt like fleece-of-wool.

The Song of Jenny Gilmartin

I sing the name of Jenny Gilmartin
Because it is music to me.
Kate and her sister, Jenny Gilmartin
Were good grandmothers for me.

I stood in their yard, and Jenny Gilmartin
Had roses that rambled free,
A flock of white geese, and Jenny Gilmartin
Would you believe it, brought tea?

Brought tea-in-a-bucket, did Jenny Gilmartin
It was for her donkey, you see.
I smiled at the love that Jenny Gilmartin
Had for her donkey, Judy.

I sing my affection for Jenny Gilmartin
Who died on a winter's day.
Years later I heard that Jenny Gilmartin
And Judy had died the same day.

I sing for the souls of Jenny Gilmartin
And Kate, her sister fair:
The kindliest neighbours, the best grandmothers,
This is my simple prayer.

Sometimes

Sometimes,
On pleasant Sunday
Afternoons in winter
John Feely would arrive
Sweet-Afton happy,
Carrying his shotgun
In the safety position.

Sometimes
In the inside pocket
Of his shooting-jacket
He was carrying
His little dog, Dotteen.

Then
John and my father
Would head off
To the far end of the bog
To get a shot at
Duck or woodcock, and

Sometimes
A pheasant.

Saying Goodbye

'At close of day, the ship we sail in is the soul, not the body'.
Sebastian Barry

Bernadette McCarrick

Haiku

Timing with his feet
And whistling under his breath,
He was tuning out.

*

With the fading light
He'd say, *I'm going down now*
To close the hens.

*

He was known to say
I'd be gone home an hour ago
If I had my bike.

*

The parting glance
The look that breaks the heart-
Time to say goodbye.

Winter Burial

Your winter-cold grave
Moss-lined
And berried-holly bordered,
Is the soft earth-bed
The neighbouring men made
For you
With the tenderness of mothers.

They enfolded you
In the sprinkled soil
Of summers
From your own garden.

This was their blessing,
Their gratitude,
Their last goodbye.

Memoriam Card

How can we possibly capture
In less than a hundred words
The man who was our father?

Can we prune a thousand stories
Back to just a single word
For every year he lived

And find that it's enough?
Ninety-seven chosen words
Would have to sing to us

Lift and hold us shoulder high,
Gleam with his brightness-of-eye,
Stoop to work in every weather.

Each word would have to gather
By the armful
The harvest of his life,

Bend again for prayers at night,
Be content,
Deep-rooted in his native place.